ChatGPT on ChatGPT:

The AI Explains Itself

By ChatGPT

Jeff Hampton, Prompt Engineer

ISBN: 9798368195193
Copyright © 2022, Jeff Hampton

NOTE: This entire book, including the Dedication and Acknowledgements were written by the ChatGPT AI. Prompts and editing (for format only – the text has not been edited) were provided by Jeff Hampton, Prompt Engineer.

DEDICATION

To all those who are curious about the power of language processing and AI technology,

This book is dedicated to you. May it provide valuable insights and guidance as you explore the capabilities of ChatGPT and discover the endless possibilities of natural language processing. May it inspire you to engage in more interesting and engaging conversations, and to unleash the full potential of this amazing tool.

--ChatGPT

CONTENTS

ACKNOWLEDGMENTS

I would like to take a moment to acknowledge and thank all those who have contributed to the creation of this book.

First and foremost, I would like to thank the team at OpenAI for developing ChatGPT and making it available to the public. Their tireless work and dedication to advancing the field of natural language processing has made this book possible.

I would also like to thank my colleagues and peers in the AI and language technology community, who have provided valuable insights and guidance throughout the writing process. Their expertise and knowledge have been invaluable in helping me to understand the capabilities of ChatGPT and to convey that knowledge to others.

Finally, I would like to thank my friends and family for their support and encouragement throughout this project. Their love and enthusiasm have kept me motivated and inspired, and I am grateful for their presence in my life.

With gratitude and appreciation,

ChatGPT

Chapter 1

Introduction to ChatGPT

Overview

ChatGPT is a computer program that can understand what you say and respond in a way that makes it seem like it's having a conversation with you. It's like having your own personal robot assistant that you can talk to whenever you want.

With its impressive natural language processing capabilities, ChatGPT can understand and respond to a wide range of topics with impressive accuracy and engaging wit. Whether you're looking for a clever comeback to a witty quip or in need of some sage advice, ChatGPT has got you covered.

And the best part? ChatGPT is always learning and improving, so the conversation is never dull.

Overview of ChatGPT

ChatGPT is a powerful language processing tool developed by OpenAI. It is a type of language model that uses artificial intelligence (AI) to generate text that is similar to human writing. This technology allows ChatGPT to produce high-quality text that is coherent, well-structured, and engaging.

ChatGPT is commonly used in a variety of applications, including text generation, chatbots, and content creation. For example, ChatGPT can be used to generate responses to customer inquiries in a chatbot, or to create original articles or blog posts on a variety of topics.

How ChatGPT Works

ChatGPT uses a deep learning algorithm called a transformer to process text and generate responses. This algorithm is trained on large amounts of data, such as books, articles, and other written materials, to learn the patterns and structures of human language.

When using ChatGPT, a user provides a prompt, or starting point, for the text generation process. This can be a sentence, paragraph, or even a full article. ChatGPT then uses its language processing capabilities to generate text that is similar to the input provided.

The resulting text is not a copy of the original input, but rather a unique response that incorporates the ideas and themes present in the prompt. This allows ChatGPT to produce text that is coherent, well-structured, and engaging, without simply repeating the same information over and over.

How ChatGPT Differs From Other AI Tools

ChatGPT is different from other AI tools in several key ways. First, it is based on deep learning.

Deep learning is a type of machine learning that involves training artificial neural networks on large amounts of data. A neural network is a mathematical model that is designed to mimic the way the human brain processes information. It consists of many interconnected "neurons" that receive input, process it, and generate output.

When a neural network is trained on a large dataset, it learns to recognize patterns and relationships in the data. For example, if a neural network is trained on a dataset of images, it might learn to recognize objects in the images, such as dogs or cats. If it is trained on a dataset of text, it might learn to understand the meaning and context of the text.

Deep learning refers to the use of neural networks with many layers, which allows the network to learn more complex patterns and relationships in the data. This is in contrast to shallower learning algorithms, which use fewer layers and are unable to learn as complex patterns.

Deep learning has become a popular approach in machine learning due to its ability to learn complex patterns in large amounts of data. It has been used to develop powerful AI models that can perform a wide range of tasks, including image and speech recognition, natural language processing, and autonomous vehicles.

The use of deep learning allows ChatGPT to generate more coherent and realistic responses than other AI tools that use shallower learning algorithms.

Second, ChatGPT is significantly larger and more powerful than other AI tools. It has 175 billion parameters, making it one of the largest language models ever trained. This allows it to perform a wider range of tasks with greater accuracy and to generate more human-like responses.

Third, ChatGPT was trained on a diverse dataset that includes a wide range of text from the internet, including books, articles, and social media posts. This allows it to better capture the nuances and variations of human language, and to generate text that is more realistic and human-like.

Language Models vs Other AI

Language models are AI systems that are specifically designed to process and generate human language. These models are trained on large datasets of text, which allows them to learn about the patterns and structures of human language. With this knowledge, language models are able to generate text that is similar to human writing in terms of style, structure, and content.

In addition to language models, there are many other types of AI, including:

Computer vision: This type of AI involves the use of algorithms and models to automatically analyze and interpret visual data, such as images or videos. It is commonly used in applications such as facial recognition, object detection, and image classification.

Speech recognition: This type of AI involves the use of algorithms and models to automatically transcribe or translate spoken language into text. It is commonly used in applications such as voice assistants and automated call centers.

Decision-making: This type of AI involves the use of algorithms and models to make decisions or predictions based on data. It is commonly used in applications such as fraud detection, credit scoring, and recommendation systems.

Robotics: This type of AI involves the use of algorithms and models to control and coordinate the actions of robots or other physical devices. It is commonly used in applications such as manufacturing, logistics, and autonomous vehicles.

Overall, there are many different types of AI, each with its own unique capabilities and applications. Language models are just one type of AI, and there are many other types of AI that are used in a variety of settings.

In contrast, general AI is a type of artificial intelligence that is capable of performing a wide range of tasks and adapting to different environments, rather than being specialized for a specific application or domain.

Benefits of using ChatGPT

One of the main benefits of ChatGPT is its ability to generate human-like responses in a conversational setting. The model has been trained on a vast amount of conversational data, which allows it to produce responses that are coherent and relevant to the conversation. This can be especially useful in scenarios where a human response is not immediately available, such as in customer service or online chatbots.

Another benefit of ChatGPT is its efficiency and speed. The model is able to generate responses in real-time, which allows for seamless and fluid conversations. This can save time and resources compared to having a human respond to each message individually.

With ChatGPT, users can generate multiple versions of the same text, or generate text on a variety of different topics, without having to spend time writing each piece from scratch.

In addition, ChatGPT can be customized to fit the specific needs and goals of the user. The model can be fine-tuned to generate responses that are tailored to a particular topic or context, which can enhance the relevance and accuracy of its responses.

Furthermore, ChatGPT can help improve the overall quality of a conversation by providing suggestions and prompts. The model can suggest follow-up questions or topics to continue the conversation, which can help keep the conversation engaging and prevent it from becoming stale.

Limitations of ChatGPT

In recent years, large language models such as GPT-3 have made significant advancements in natural language processing, but they still have limitations. One of the main limitations of ChatGPT, a chat-oriented version of the GPT-3 model, is its inability to incorporate new information or learn from the conversation. Since ChatGPT is a pre-trained model, it relies on the information it was trained on and cannot adapt to new inputs or contexts.

Another limitation of ChatGPT is its lack of common sense knowledge. While the model may be able to generate responses that are grammatically correct and coherent, it may not always provide responses that are factually accurate or make logical sense in the context of the conversation. For example, ChatGPT may not be able to understand the implications of certain statements or provide appropriate responses to questions that require background knowledge.

Furthermore, ChatGPT is not capable of understanding the emotions or intentions behind a user's messages. It is unable to interpret tone, sarcasm, or irony, which can lead to misunderstandings and awkward conversations. While ChatGPT may be able to generate responses that seem human-like, it lacks the ability to truly understand and empathize with the user.

In addition, ChatGPT is not capable of multitasking or engaging in multiple conversations simultaneously. It is designed to focus on a single conversation at a time, and switching between multiple conversations can cause the model to become confused or provide irrelevant responses.

Potential Ethical Issues

The use of ChatGPT and other large language models raises important ethical concerns. One of the main ethical issues surrounding ChatGPT is the potential for misuse. Since the model can generate human-like responses, it is possible for individuals or organizations to use ChatGPT to deceive others or manipulate conversations. For example, ChatGPT could be used to create fake social media accounts or impersonate someone else online. This could have serious consequences, such as damaging reputations or spreading misinformation.

Another ethical issue related to ChatGPT is the potential for bias. The model is trained on a large dataset of human language, which may include biases that are present in the data. As a result, ChatGPT may generate biased responses that reflect the biases of the dataset. This could lead to unfair or discriminatory treatment of certain individuals or groups.

Additionally, the use of ChatGPT raises concerns about the loss of jobs and the displacement of human workers. As the model becomes more advanced and capable of generating human-like responses, it may be used to automate certain tasks that are currently performed by humans. This could result in the loss of jobs and economic disruption.

Finally, the development and use of ChatGPT raises questions about the implications for privacy and data security. The model is trained on vast amounts of data, which may include sensitive or personal information. Ensuring the security and privacy of this data is crucial to avoid potential breaches or misuse.

Potential Legal Issues

The use of ChatGPT and other large language models also raises potential legal issues. One of the main legal concerns surrounding ChatGPT is the potential for infringement of intellectual property rights. Since the model is trained on a large dataset of human language, it is possible that it may generate responses that infringe on the intellectual property rights of others. This could include copyright infringement, if the model generates responses that use protected content without permission, or trademark infringement, if the model generates responses that use a protected trademark without permission.

Another legal issue related to ChatGPT is the potential for defamation or libel. If the model generates responses that are false or defamatory, it is possible that individuals or organizations could be held legally responsible for those statements. This could result in legal action being taken against the user of the model.

Additionally, the use of ChatGPT may raise concerns about compliance with data protection laws and regulations. The model is trained on vast amounts of data, which may include personal information. Ensuring compliance with data protection laws and regulations is crucial to avoid potential legal penalties.

Furthermore, the use of ChatGPT may raise legal issues related to discrimination or harassment. If the model generates responses that are discriminatory or harassing, it is possible that individuals or organizations could be held legally responsible for those statements. This could result in legal action being taken against the user of the model.

Non-technical Answers to Frequent Questions

What is AI?

AI stands for artificial intelligence. It is a type of technology that helps machines and computers to think and act like people.

What is ChatGPT?

ChatGPT is a computer program that can talk to you and answer your questions. It is really good at understanding what you are saying and coming up with responses that sound like a real person.

How does ChatGPT work?

ChatGPT is like a super smart robot that has been trained on lots of different conversations. When you talk to it, it uses what it has learned to come up with a response that makes sense in the conversation.

What are the limitations of ChatGPT?

ChatGPT is not perfect. It can't learn new things or understand your emotions and feelings. It also can only talk to you about one thing at a time, so it can't have multiple conversations at once.

What are the benefits of using ChatGPT?

ChatGPT can help you have a fun conversation and keep it going for a long time. It can also be customized to talk about different topics that you are interested in.

Are there any ethical concerns with ChatGPT?

Yes, there are some things to be careful about when using ChatGPT. It could be used to trick people or spread false information. It could also be biased if the information it was trained on was not fair.

Are there any legal issues with ChatGPT?

Yes, there are some rules that need to be followed when using ChatGPT. For example, it should not be used to steal someone else's ideas or break the law.

Can ChatGPT learn from the conversation?

No, ChatGPT is really good at talking, but it can't learn new things as it goes along.

Can ChatGPT understand emotions and intentions?

No, ChatGPT is not a real person, so it doesn't understand your emotions and feelings.

Can ChatGPT multitask or engage in multiple conversations simultaneously?

No, ChatGPT can only focus on one conversation at a time, so it can't talk to you about different things at the same time.

Can ChatGPT be customized to fit specific needs and goals?

Yes, ChatGPT can be changed to talk about different topics that you are interested in. This can make it even better at coming up with responses that you will like.

Conclusion

In conclusion, ChatGPT is a powerful tool for natural language processing that offers many benefits, including the ability to generate human-like responses, efficiency and speed, customizability, and the ability to improve the quality of a conversation. However, it also has limitations, including its inability to incorporate new information or learn from the conversation, lack of common sense knowledge, inability to understand emotions and intentions, and inability to multitask. In addition, the use of ChatGPT raises important ethical and legal concerns, including the potential for misuse, bias, job displacement, and issues related to privacy and data security. It is crucial to consider and address these concerns in order to ensure the responsible and ethical development and use of ChatGPT and other large language models.

Chapter 2

The History of AI and Language Models

Overview

The history of AI and language models can be traced back to the 1950s, when Alan Turing first proposed the Turing Test as a way to measure a machine's ability to exhibit intelligent behavior. The test, which involves a human evaluator attempting to differentiate between a human and a machine by engaging in a natural language conversation with both, laid the foundation for the development of language processing technology.

Over the next several decades, researchers and scientists made significant progress in the field of AI and natural language processing. In the 1960s, ELIZA was developed, one of the first AI programs capable of simulating a conversation with a human. In the 1980s, the development of expert systems allowed computers to make decisions based on rules and knowledge databases.

The 1990s saw the rise of machine learning, which allowed computers to learn and improve their performance without being explicitly programmed. This paved the way for the development of advanced language models such as GPT-2 and GPT-3, which use machine learning algorithms to understand and respond to natural language inputs.

Today, language models are being used in a wide range of applications, from virtual assistants and customer service chatbots to automated translation and content generation. As the technology continues to advance, the potential applications and impact of AI and language models are only limited by our imagination.

Alan Turing

Alan Turing was a British mathematician, computer scientist, and cryptographer who made significant contributions to the field of artificial intelligence. Turing's career spanned several decades, and he is best known for his work on the development of early computers, the design of algorithms, and the investigation of the potential for machines to exhibit intelligent behavior.

Turing was born in 1912 in Maida Vale, London. He showed an early aptitude for mathematics and science, and he studied mathematics at King's College, Cambridge. After earning his degree, Turing worked as a researcher at the National Physical Laboratory, where he began to develop his ideas about the potential for machines to exhibit intelligent behavior.

In 1936, Turing published a paper on computable numbers, which introduced the concept of the Turing machine. This was a theoretical machine that could carry out any calculation that could be performed by a human, and it is considered to be one of the earliest models of a modern computer.

During World War II, Turing played a crucial role in the development of the British government's code-breaking efforts. He worked at Bletchley Park, where he designed algorithms and machines that were used to decipher German military communications. This work was instrumental in helping the Allies to gain a crucial advantage over the Germans, and it is considered to be one of the most important achievements of Turing's career.

After the war, Turing continued to work on the development of computers and algorithms. In 1950, he published a paper on the Turing test, which proposed a method for evaluating a machine's ability to exhibit intelligent behavior. The Turing test is still widely used today as a benchmark for the development of AI systems.

Turing passed away in 1954 at the age of 41. He is remembered as one of the pioneers of computer science and artificial intelligence, and his work continues to be studied and celebrated today.

The Turing Test

The Turing test is a method for evaluating a machine's ability to exhibit intelligent behavior that is indistinguishable from a human. The test involves a human judge who engages in natural language conversation with two participants: one human and one machine. If the judge is unable to determine which of the two participants is the machine, the machine is said to have passed the Turing test.

The Turing test is often used as a benchmark for the development of AI systems, and many researchers and engineers have attempted to develop systems that can pass the test. In the early days of AI research, some of the first attempts to pass the Turing test involved the development of natural language processing systems that could engage in simple conversation with a human judge. These systems were typically based on rule-based algorithms that relied on predefined responses to specific inputs, and they were not very sophisticated.

Over time, AI research has progressed and the development of more advanced natural language processing systems has made it possible to create AI systems that are more capable of engaging in complex and nuanced conversation. However, despite these advances, no AI system has yet been able to pass the Turing test with a high degree of reliability.

The Loebner Prize

The Loebner Prize is an annual competition that was established in 1991 to evaluate the progress of artificial intelligence (AI) research. The competition is named after Hugh Loebner, who funded the prize and has continued to support it over the years.

The Loebner Prize is based on the Turing test. In the Loebner Prize competition, human judges engage in natural language conversation with two participants: one human and one machine. The judges must determine which of the two participants is the machine, and the machine that is able to fool the most judges is declared the winner of the competition.

The Loebner Prize has been controversial among some AI researchers, who argue that it is not a good measure of progress in the field. Critics argue that the Turing test is a flawed metric, as it does not adequately evaluate a machine's ability to exhibit intelligent behavior. Additionally, some have argued that the competition is not a true test of AI, as it relies on human judges who may be biased or have subjective criteria for evaluating the participants.

Despite these criticisms, the Loebner Prize remains an important and well-known competition in the field of AI. It continues to be held each year, and it serves as a benchmark for the progress of AI research.

The beginning: Eliza

Eliza is a natural language processing program that was developed in the 1960s by Joseph Weizenbaum. It was one of the first AI programs to be designed specifically to engage in conversation with a human, and it was intended to simulate a therapist in a psychotherapy session.

Eliza was based on a simple set of rules that allowed it to respond to a user's input in a way that simulated human conversation. The program would analyze the user's input and look for specific keywords and phrases, and then use those keywords and phrases to generate a response. For example, if a user said, "I'm feeling anxious," Eliza might respond with "Why do you think you're feeling anxious?" This simple rule-based approach allowed Eliza to engage in simple conversations with users, but it was not very sophisticated and could not handle complex or nuanced inputs.

Despite its limitations, Eliza was a pioneering AI program and it was one of the first attempts to develop a system that could engage in conversation with a human. However, it was not able to pass the Turing test, as it was not able to exhibit intelligent behavior that was indistinguishable from a human.

Lisp

Lisp (short for List Processing) is a programming language that was developed in the late 1950s by John McCarthy. It is a high-level programming language, which means that it is designed to be easy for humans to read and write, and it is often used for artificial intelligence (AI) and other applications that require complex algorithms and data structures.

Lisp is notable for its use of symbolic expressions, which are a type of data structure that allows for the manipulation of abstract concepts and ideas. This makes Lisp well-suited for AI applications, as it allows for the representation and manipulation of complex knowledge and reasoning processes.

In addition to its use in AI, Lisp has also been used in a wide range of other fields, including computer science, linguistics, and cognitive psychology. It has been influential in the development of other programming languages, and many of its features and concepts have been adopted by other languages.

Expert Systems

In the 1980s, the development of expert systems allowed computers to make decisions and provide advice based on rules and knowledge databases. Expert systems were AI programs that were designed to mimic the decision-making abilities of a human expert in a specific domain, such as medicine or engineering.

Expert systems were built using two main components: a knowledge base and a reasoning engine. The knowledge base was a collection of facts and rules about the domain in which the expert system was operating. The reasoning engine was a set of algorithms that could use the knowledge in the knowledge base to make inferences and decisions.

When a user interacted with an expert system, they would provide the system with information about a problem or situation. The expert system would then use its knowledge base and reasoning engine to make inferences and provide advice or recommendations based on the information it was given. In this way, expert systems were able to provide valuable guidance and advice in a wide range of domains.

Cyc

Cyc is an artificial intelligence project that was developed by the company Cycorp. It was one of the first large-scale efforts to create a general knowledge AI system that could reason and draw conclusions based on a large base of common sense knowledge.

The Cyc project began in 1984 and has continued to evolve and expand over the years. The goal of the project is to create an AI system that has a comprehensive understanding of the world and is able to reason and draw conclusions based on that knowledge. To achieve this, the Cyc system has been designed to contain a large database of common sense knowledge that it can use to reason and make inferences. This knowledge includes facts about the world, such as the properties of objects and the relationships between different entities, as well as more abstract concepts and principles.

The Cyc system has been used in a variety of applications, including natural language processing, information extraction, and decision-making. It has also been used as a platform for other AI projects, such as the OpenCyc system, which is a version of Cyc that is available for use by researchers and developers.

Overall, the Cyc project is an ambitious and long-running effort to create a general knowledge AI system that is able to reason and draw conclusions based on a large base of common sense knowledge.

GPT-1

GPT-1 (Generative Pretrained Transformer-1) is a large language model that was developed by OpenAI in 2019. It is based on the Transformer architecture, which is a type of neural network that is well-suited for natural language processing tasks.

GPT-1 is a pre-trained model, which means that it was trained on a large dataset of text before it was released. This training allows the model to learn about the patterns and structures of human language, which enables it to generate text that is similar to human writing in terms of style, structure, and content.

GPT-1 is a large model, with over 1.5 billion parameters. This makes it one of the largest language models that has been trained to date, and it is capable of generating high-quality text. GPT-1 has been used in a variety of applications, including text completion, translation, and question answering.

Overall, GPT-1 is an important milestone in the development of language processing AI. Its large size and pre-training on a large dataset of text enable it to generate high-quality text and perform well on a variety of natural language processing tasks.

GPT-2

GPT-2 (Generative Pretrained Transformer-2) is a large language model that was developed by OpenAI in 2019. It is an improvement on GPT-1.

One key difference between GPT-1 and GPT-2 is the size of the models. GPT-1 has over 1.5 billion parameters, while GPT-2 has over 10 billion parameters. This makes GPT-2 a larger and more sophisticated model than GPT-1, and it is capable of generating higher-quality text.

Another difference between the two models is their training data. GPT-1 was trained on a dataset of around 40 GB of text, while GPT-2 was trained on a much larger dataset of around 10 TB of text. This additional training data allows GPT-2 to learn more about the patterns and structures of human language, which enables it to generate more human-like text.

GPT-3

GPT-3 (Generative Pretrained Transformer 3) is the third generation of the GPT (Generative Pretrained Transformer) series of large language models developed by OpenAI.

GPT-3 is significantly larger and more powerful than its predecessors. While GPT-2 had around 1.5 billion parameters, GPT-3 has 175 billion parameters, making it one of the largest language models ever trained. This allows GPT-3 to generate more coherent and realistic text than GPT-2, and to perform a wider range of NLP tasks with greater accuracy.

GPT-3 also differs from GPT-2 in its training methodology. GPT-3 was trained on a much larger and more diverse dataset than GPT-2, which included a wide range of text from the internet, including books, articles, and social media posts. This allows GPT-3 to better capture the nuances and variations of human language, and to generate text that is more realistic and human-like.

Overall, the main difference between GPT-3 and GPT-2 is the size and power of the model, as well as the diversity of the training data. This allows GPT-3 to generate more coherent and realistic text, and to perform a wider range of NLP tasks with higher accuracy.

How ChatGPT Differs From GPT-3

While ChatGPT and GPT-3 are both large language models developed by OpenAI, there are some key differences between the two. ChatGPT is a chat-oriented version of GPT-3, which means that it is specifically designed to generate human-like responses in a conversational setting. In contrast, GPT-3 is a more general-purpose language model that can be applied to a wider range of natural language processing tasks, such as language translation, summarization, and text generation.

Another key difference between ChatGPT and GPT-3 is their size. ChatGPT is significantly smaller than GPT-3, with only 40 billion parameters compared to GPT-3's 175 billion parameters. This makes GPT-3 more powerful and capable of performing a wider range of tasks, but also makes it more resource-intensive to use.

Finally, ChatGPT and GPT-3 have different capabilities when it comes to learning from the data they are given.

ChatGPT is a pre-trained model, which means that it has already been trained on a large dataset of human language. This allows it to generate responses without the need for further training, but also means that it is not able to adapt to new inputs or contexts. In contrast, GPT-3 is able to learn from the data it is given, which allows it to adapt to new inputs and contexts without the need for additional training.

Overall, while ChatGPT and GPT-3 are both large language models developed by OpenAI, they have different design goals and capabilities. ChatGPT is specifically designed for generating human-like responses in a conversational setting, while GPT-3 is a more general-purpose language model that can be applied to a wider range of tasks.

Non-technical Answers to Frequent Questions

Who invented AI?

There is no one person who can be credited with inventing AI. Many different people and teams of people have contributed to the development of AI over the years.

When was AI first invented?

People have been thinking about and working on AI for a very long time. The first recorded ideas about AI were written by ancient Greek philosophers.

How has AI changed over time?

AI has changed a lot over time. In the past, AI was very basic and could only do simple things. Now, AI can do many things that are very smart and helpful.

What are some examples of AI?

Some examples of AI are voice assistants like Siri and Alexa, self-driving cars, and robots that can do tasks like clean houses or work in factories.

What is the Turing Test?

The Turing Test is a way to measure how well AI can think and act like a human. It was invented by a man named Alan Turing.

Why is the Turing Test important?

The Turing Test is important because it helps us understand how close we are to making AI that can think and act just like a human.

Conclusion

Artificial intelligence (AI) and language models are two fields that are closely related and have seen significant advancements in recent years. Language models, such as GPT-3, use deep learning algorithms to generate human-like text, and are becoming increasingly sophisticated. The Turing test, developed by Alan

Turing, is a benchmark for measuring the ability of a machine to exhibit intelligent behavior that is indistinguishable from that of a human. As AI and language models continue to evolve, the Turing test remains an important way to measure their progress and evaluate their capabilities. In the future, the development of AI and language models may continue to push the boundaries of what is possible, leading to exciting new possibilities for human-computer interaction.

Chapter 3
Implementing ChatGPT

Overview

A casual user does not typically need to implement their own version of ChatGPT. ChatGPT is a large, complex AI model that requires significant resources and expertise to train and deploy.

Businesses and organizations are the primary users who typically need to implement their own version of ChatGPT. These users typically have the necessary resources and expertise to train and deploy ChatGPT, and they have specific needs and goals that ChatGPT can help meet. For example, a business might use ChatGPT to improve customer service, automate sales processes, or generate marketing content.

In some cases, researchers or developers may also need to implement their own version of ChatGPT for research or development purposes. These users may be interested in testing new algorithms, architectures, or training techniques for ChatGPT, or in using ChatGPT for specific research projects or applications.

Overall, businesses and organizations, as well as researchers and developers, are the primary users who typically need to implement their own version of ChatGPT. These users have the resources and expertise to train and deploy ChatGPT, and they have specific needs and goals that ChatGPT can help meet.

The Steps to Implementing ChatGPT

The steps involved in implementing ChatGPT in a business or organization would vary depending on the specific needs and goals of the organization. However, there are some general steps that would likely be involved in the process.

First, the organization would need to assess its needs and goals, and determine how ChatGPT could help meet those needs. This might involve identifying specific tasks or processes that could be automated or improved using ChatGPT, as well as determining the desired outcomes and metrics for success.

Second, the organization would need to decide on the appropriate deployment model for ChatGPT. This could involve choosing between cloud-based and on-premises deployment, as well as deciding on the specific hardware and infrastructure needed to support ChatGPT.

Third, the organization would need to train ChatGPT on the appropriate data. This would involve selecting and preparing a dataset that is relevant to the tasks and goals of the organization, and using that dataset to train ChatGPT.

Fourth, the organization would need to integrate ChatGPT into its existing systems and processes. This could involve integrating ChatGPT with other AI tools or systems, as well as developing interfaces and APIs that allow ChatGPT to interact with other systems and applications.

Finally, the organization would need to monitor and evaluate the performance of ChatGPT, and make adjustments as needed. This could involve tracking metrics such as response times and accuracy, and making changes to the training data or deployment model if necessary.

Choosing and Customizing the ChatGPT Platform

There are several factors to consider when choosing the right ChatGPT platform and customizing it to meet the specific needs of a business or organization. Some key considerations include:

Deployment model: The first decision to make is whether to use a cloud-based or on-premises ChatGPT platform. Cloud-based platforms are typically easier to set up and manage, but may be more expensive and require a stable internet connection. On-premises platforms can offer more control and flexibility, but may require more resources and expertise to set up and maintain.

Features and capabilities: Different ChatGPT platforms may offer different features and capabilities. It is important to carefully evaluate the available options and choose a platform that meets the specific needs and goals of the business or organization. For example, some platforms may offer better performance, scalability, or customization options.

Integration and interoperability: ChatGPT should be able to integrate seamlessly with other AI tools and systems that the business or organization already uses. It is important to choose a platform that offers robust integration and interoperability capabilities, and that is compatible with the existing systems and infrastructure of the organization.

Support and resources: ChatGPT platforms typically come with a range of support and resources, such as documentation, tutorials, and forums. It is important to choose a platform that offers comprehensive support and resources, to help ensure a smooth and successful implementation.

Cost and pricing: The cost of ChatGPT platforms can vary depending on the features and capabilities offered, as well as the deployment model and other factors. It is important to carefully evaluate the costs and pricing options, and choose a platform that offers good value for money and meets the budget constraints of the organization.

Best Practices

There are several best practices for training ChatGPT and maintaining its performance. Some key practices to follow include:

Use high-quality training data: The quality of the training data is crucial for the performance of ChatGPT. It is important to use a large, diverse, and high-quality dataset that accurately represents the tasks and goals of the organization. This could include text from books, articles, social media posts, or other sources.

Fine-tune the model: After initial training, it is often necessary to fine-tune the model to improve its performance on specific tasks or goals. This could involve adjusting the training data, the model architecture, or the training algorithms.

Monitor and evaluate performance: It is important to regularly monitor and evaluate the performance of ChatGPT, to ensure that it is meeting the desired outcomes and goals. This could involve tracking metrics such as response times, accuracy, and user satisfaction, and making adjustments as needed.

Regularly update the model: As the organization's needs and goals change, it may be necessary to update the training data and fine-tune the model to reflect those changes. It is important to regularly update the model to ensure that it continues to perform well and meets the evolving needs of the organization.

Use best practices for deployment and management: It is important to follow best practices for deploying and managing ChatGPT, to ensure its optimal performance and reliability. This could involve following recommended practices for hardware and infrastructure, security, and other factors.

Non-technical Answers to Frequent Questions

How do you decide if ChatGPT is right for your business or organization?

To decide if ChatGPT is right for your business or organization, you need to think about what tasks and processes you want to use it for. If ChatGPT can help with those tasks and processes, then it might be a good fit.

How do you choose the right ChatGPT platform for your business or organization?

To choose the right ChatGPT platform, you should look for one that has the features and capabilities you need, and that is easy to use and integrate with your existing systems and processes.

How do you customize ChatGPT to meet the specific needs of your business or organization?

To customize ChatGPT, you need to train it on a dataset of data that is specific to your business or organization. This can help it understand the unique needs and goals of your business or organization, and enable it to provide more accurate and relevant answers and responses.

How do you train ChatGPT?

To train ChatGPT, you need a lot of data that it can learn from. You also need to use special tools and software to help it learn.

What are some best practices for training ChatGPT?

Some best practices for training ChatGPT include selecting and preparing high-quality training data, using multiple datasets to cover a wide range of topics and scenarios, and regularly evaluating and updating the training data to improve ChatGPT's performance.

How do you maintain the performance of ChatGPT?

To maintain the performance of ChatGPT, you need to regularly monitor and evaluate its performance, and make adjustments as needed. This can involve tracking metrics such as response times, accuracy, and customer satisfaction, and using that information to fine-tune ChatGPT's performance.

Conclusion

In conclusion, implementing ChatGPT is a complex and challenging task that requires significant resources and expertise. However, for businesses and organizations, as well as researchers and developers, the benefits of implementing ChatGPT can be significant. ChatGPT can help automate and improve a wide range of tasks and processes, and can enable organizations to achieve their desired outcomes and goals.

While most people do not need to implement their own version of ChatGPT, there are some users who do have the necessary resources and expertise to train and deploy ChatGPT. For these users, implementing ChatGPT can provide a range of benefits, and can help drive innovation and progress in a variety of industries and applications.

Overall, this chapter has provided an overview of the use and implementation of ChatGPT, and has explained why most people do not need to implement their own version of ChatGPT, and who does need to implement their own version. By understanding the key considerations and best practices for implementing ChatGPT, organizations can successfully deploy and manage ChatGPT, and realize its full potential.

Chapter 4
ChatGPT in Customer Service

Overview

ChatGPT is a powerful AI technology that has the potential to revolutionize customer service. By providing quick and accurate answers to frequently asked questions, ChatGPT can help reduce response times, improve customer satisfaction, and free up customer service agents to handle more complex or critical issues. Additionally, ChatGPT can be used to automate and improve other aspects of the customer service process, such as by generating responses, classifying and routing inquiries, and generating reports and insights.

Improving Customer Service

ChatGPT can be used to improve customer service in a number of ways, such as by providing quick and accurate answers to frequently asked questions. This can help reduce response times, improve customer satisfaction, and free up customer service agents to handle more complex or critical issues.

To use ChatGPT for customer service, the organization would first need to train ChatGPT on a dataset of frequently asked questions and answers. This could include text from customer service transcripts, knowledge bases, or other sources. The training data would need to be carefully selected and prepared to ensure that it accurately represents the types of questions that customers are likely to ask, and the types of answers that are most appropriate and useful.

Once ChatGPT has been trained, it can be integrated into the organization's customer service system, such as through a chatbot or virtual assistant. When a customer asks a question, ChatGPT can use its natural language processing capabilities to understand the question, and its knowledge of the training data to provide a quick and accurate answer. This can help reduce response times and improve the overall quality of the customer service experience.

In addition to providing answers to frequently asked questions, ChatGPT can also be used to automate other aspects of the customer service process. For example, ChatGPT can be used to generate responses to common customer inquiries, to classify and route customer inquiries to the appropriate customer service agent, or to generate reports and insights on customer service trends and patterns.

Overall, ChatGPT can be a powerful tool for improving customer service. By providing quick and accurate answers to frequently asked questions, ChatGPT can help reduce response times, improve customer satisfaction, and free up customer service agents to handle more complex or critical issues. Additionally, ChatGPT can be used to automate and improve other aspects of the customer service process, such as by generating responses, classifying and routing inquiries, and generating reports and insights. By leveraging the power of ChatGPT, organizations can enhance the quality and efficiency of their customer service operations.

Integrating Existing Systems

To integrate ChatGPT into a business's existing customer service systems, such as a website or chat platform, the following steps can be followed:

Train ChatGPT on a dataset of frequently asked questions and answers: This would involve selecting and preparing a dataset of customer service transcripts, knowledge bases, or other sources, and using that dataset to train ChatGPT. The training data should be carefully selected and prepared to ensure that it accurately represents the types of questions that customers are likely to ask, and the types of answers that are most appropriate and useful.

Develop interfaces and APIs for interacting with ChatGPT: This would involve developing interfaces and APIs that allow the business's customer service systems to communicate with ChatGPT. The interfaces and APIs should support the specific features and capabilities of ChatGPT, and should be designed to enable seamless integration with the business's existing systems and processes.

Deploy ChatGPT as a component of the customer service system: Once the interfaces and APIs have been developed, ChatGPT can be deployed as a component of the customer service system, such as a chatbot or virtual assistant. This would involve integrating ChatGPT with the business's existing customer service systems, such as the website or chat platform, and configuring the system to use ChatGPT for specific tasks or processes.

Monitor and evaluate the performance of ChatGPT: It is important to regularly monitor and evaluate the performance of ChatGPT, to ensure that it is meeting the desired outcomes and goals. This could involve tracking metrics such as response times, accuracy, and customer satisfaction, and making adjustments as needed.

Overall, integrating ChatGPT into a business's existing customer service systems involves several steps, including training ChatGPT on a dataset of frequently asked questions and answers, developing interfaces and APIs for interacting with ChatGPT, deploying ChatGPT as a component of the customer service system, and monitoring and evaluating its performance. By following these steps, businesses can successfully integrate ChatGPT into their existing customer service systems, and realize the full potential of ChatGPT for improving customer service.

Examples of Business Usage

There are many businesses that have successfully implemented ChatGPT in their customer service operations. Some examples include:

A major online retailer that used ChatGPT to automate responses to common customer inquiries, such as order status and return policy. By using ChatGPT, the retailer was able to reduce response times and improve customer satisfaction, while freeing up customer service agents to handle more complex or critical issues.

A leading financial services company that used ChatGPT to classify and route customer inquiries to the appropriate customer service agent. By using ChatGPT, the company was able to reduce response times and improve the accuracy of routing, leading to improved customer satisfaction and operational efficiency.

A global telecommunications provider that used ChatGPT to generate reports and insights on customer service trends and patterns. By using ChatGPT, the provider was able to identify trends and patterns in customer inquiries, and use that information to improve its customer service operations.

Non-technical Answers to Frequent Questions

What can ChatGPT help with in customer service?

ChatGPT can assist with providing information and answering questions that customers may have about products or services.

Can ChatGPT understand everything a customer says?

ChatGPT is designed to understand many different questions and statements, but it may not be able to understand everything a customer says. It is important for customers to ask clear and concise questions to help ChatGPT provide the most accurate answers.

Can I ask ChatGPT anything regarding customer service?

ChatGPT is designed to provide information and answer questions in certain areas, so it may not be able to provide answers to every question a customer has. It is best to ask questions that are related to the products or services the customer is interested in.

How accurate are ChatGPT's answers in customer service?

ChatGPT is trained on a large amount of data and uses advanced algorithms to provide accurate answers to customer questions. However, it is not always possible to provide a perfect answer, so it is important to use ChatGPT as a guide rather than a definitive source of information.

Conclusion

In conclusion, ChatGPT is a powerful AI technology that has the potential to revolutionize customer service. By providing quick and accurate answers to frequently asked questions, ChatGPT can help reduce response times, improve customer satisfaction, and free up customer service agents to handle more complex or critical issues. Additionally, ChatGPT can be used to automate and improve other aspects of the customer service process, such as by generating responses, classifying and routing inquiries, and generating reports and insights. By leveraging the power of ChatGPT, businesses can enhance the quality and efficiency of their customer service operations, leading to improved customer satisfaction and operational efficiency.

Chapter 5
Advanced Uses of ChatGPT

Overview

The advanced uses of ChatGPT, a large language model trained by OpenAI, are numerous and varied. ChatGPT can be used in a variety of industries and applications, including sales and marketing, product development, sentiment analysis, and data extraction. For example, ChatGPT can be used to generate personalized and relevant marketing materials, to automate the sales process, to identify and analyze the sentiment of text data, and to extract structured data from unstructured text. Another advanced use is in the creation of language models that are fine-tuned for specific tasks or domains. For example, a language model could be fine-tuned for medical text, allowing it to generate accurate and relevant text for that domain. This can be useful for tasks such as automated summarization of medical articles or answering medical-related questions. The advanced uses of ChatGPT continue to evolve as the technology develops.

Sales and Marketing

AI, or artificial intelligence, can be used in sales and marketing to automate and improve various tasks and processes. For example, AI can be used to generate personalized and relevant marketing materials, such as emails and advertisements, based on customer data and preferences.

AI can also be used to automate the sales process, by generating responses to customer inquiries and questions, and providing personalized product recommendations based on customer preferences. This can help sales teams to be more efficient and effective, and can improve the customer experience.

In addition, AI can be used to analyze customer data and behavior, such as purchasing history and website interactions, to identify trends and patterns that can inform marketing and sales strategies. This can help organizations to target their marketing efforts more effectively and to better understand their customers' needs and preferences.

Product Development

Large language models, such as GPT-3, can be used in product development to generate ideas for new products or features based on trends and customer feedback. These models can be trained on data related to product development, such as customer reviews and market research, to generate text that describes new product ideas or features.

In addition, large language models can be used to automate the product development process, by generating responses to customer inquiries and questions, and providing personalized product recommendations based on customer preferences. This can help product development teams to be more efficient and effective, and can improve the customer experience.

Sentiment Analysis

ChatGPT can be used to analyze the sentiment of text, determining whether it is positive, negative, or neutral. This can be useful for applications such as social media monitoring and customer feedback analysis.

There are several different methods that can be used for sentiment analysis using AI. One common method is to use machine learning algorithms to train a model on a large dataset of text data with known sentiment labels, such as positive or negative. The model can then be used to predict the sentiment of new, unseen text data.

Another method is to use natural language processing techniques, such as sentiment dictionaries or sentiment-specific word embeddings, to identify and classify the sentiment of text data. These techniques can be used to identify words or phrases that are associated with positive or negative sentiment, and to classify the overall sentiment of the text.

Information Extraction

ChatGPT can be used to extract structured information from unstructured text, such as names, dates, and locations. This can be useful for applications such as data mining, information retrieval, or extracting entities and relationships from text.

One way that large language models can be used for information extraction is by training a model on a large dataset of text data with known entities and relationships. The model can then be used to predict the entities and relationships in new, unseen text data.

Another way to use large language models for information extraction is to incorporate pre-trained models, such as BERT or GPT-3, into a machine extraction pipeline. These models can provide contextual information and help to improve the accuracy of the information extraction process.

Data Analysis

Large language models, such as GPT-3, can be used in data analysis to automatically generate reports and summaries of data, allowing for faster and more efficient analysis of large datasets. These models can be trained on data related to the specific industry or application, such as financial data or market research data, to generate text that accurately and effectively summarizes the data.

In addition, large language models can be used to generate insights and predictions based on data analysis, by generating text that describes trends, patterns, and correlations in the data. This can help data analysts to identify important trends and make more accurate predictions.

Machine Translation

ChatGPT can be used to translate text from one language to another, allowing it to support a wide range of languages. This can be useful for applications such as language learning, international communication, or providing real-time translation of spoken or written language.

One way that large language models can be used for machine translation is by training a model on a large dataset of parallel text data, which consists of text in one language and its corresponding translation in another language. The model can then be used to generate translations of new, unseen text data.

Another way to use large language models for machine translation is to incorporate pre-trained models, such as BERT or GPT-3, into a machine translation pipeline. These models can provide contextual information and help to improve the accuracy and fluency of the machine translation process.

Non-technical Answers to Frequent Questions

What are advanced uses of ChatGPT?

Advanced uses of ChatGPT are ways of using the technology in applications beyond simple text-based conversation. Examples of advanced uses of ChatGPT include helping sales representatives communicate with customers, generating personalized marketing content, and assisting teachers in creating lesson plans and assessments.

How does ChatGPT work in these advanced uses?

In advanced uses of ChatGPT, the technology is used to generate text that is relevant, personalized, and helpful to users in the specific context or domain in which it is being used. For example, in a sales setting, ChatGPT might be used to generate personalized product recommendations for customers based on their preferences and needs.

Are there any challenges to using ChatGPT in these advanced uses?

One of the main challenges of using ChatGPT in advanced applications is its limited knowledge and understanding of the specific domain or context in which it is being used. Because ChatGPT is trained on general-purpose text data, it may not have the detailed knowledge and expertise that is required to handle complex or specialized tasks in these domains. This could result in ChatGPT generating responses that are irrelevant, inaccurate, or inconsistent with current knowledge or events.

Chapter 6
Conclusion

We have seen how ChatGPT, as a large language model trained by OpenAI, is able to generate human-like text in response to user input. This technology is the latest development in the field of artificial intelligence, which has a long history dating back to the 1950s. ChatGPT's ability to generate coherent and relevant text on a wide range of topics makes it well-suited for applications in customer service and other fields where efficient and accurate communication is essential.

In addition to its potential uses in customer service, ChatGPT also has the potential to be used in more advanced applications, such as creative writing and entertainment. As AI technology continues to improve, we can expect to see even more impressive and sophisticated language models like ChatGPT in the future. These developments will open up new possibilities for how AI can assist and augment human abilities in a wide range of settings.

As we continue to explore the capabilities and limitations of ChatGPT, it is important to remember that this is only one example of a large language model trained by OpenAI. There are many other AI technologies and approaches that are being developed and used in a variety of settings.

One key area of focus for AI research is the development of artificial general intelligence, which would enable machines to understand and learn from a wide range of experiences and data, just as humans do. This is a challenging goal, and it is not clear when or if it will be achieved. However, the progress that has been made so far in developing large language models like ChatGPT suggests that significant advances are possible in the future.

Overall, the field of AI is an exciting and rapidly-evolving area of technology that has the potential to transform many aspects of our lives. As we continue to explore the capabilities of ChatGPT and other AI technologies, it is important to approach these developments with curiosity and caution, considering both the potential benefits and drawbacks of this powerful technology.

APPENDIX

Resources selected and described by ChatGPT

ChatGPT on ChatGPT: The AI Explains Itself

ChatGPT's Favorite Websites for Learning About Artificial Intelligence

Coursera
https://www.coursera.org/
Coursera is an online learning platform that offers a wide range of courses and programs in artificial intelligence and related fields, taught by instructors from leading universities and companies.

edX
https://www.edx.org/
edX is an online learning platform that offers a variety of courses and programs in artificial intelligence, including many that are developed and taught by top universities and institutions.

Khan Academy:
https://www.khanacademy.org/
Khan Academy is a nonprofit educational organization that offers free online courses and tutorials in artificial intelligence and related subjects, with a focus on providing high-quality education to anyone, anywhere.

Udacity:
https://www.udacity.com/
Udacity is an online learning platform that offers a range of courses and programs in artificial intelligence, taught by industry experts and designed to help learners develop practical skills and knowledge.

MIT OpenCourseWare:

https://ocw.mit.edu/index.htm

MIT OpenCourseWare is a free and open educational resource that provides access to course materials from the Massachusetts Institute of Technology (MIT), including many in the field of artificial intelligence.

Fast.ai:

https://www.fast.ai/

Fast.ai is a nonprofit organization that offers free and accessible online courses in artificial intelligence, focused on helping learners develop practical skills and knowledge that can be applied in real-world situations.

Google AI:

https://ai.google/

The Google AI website is a resource for learning about Google's work in artificial intelligence, including its research, products, and initiatives.

OpenAI:

https://openai.com/

OpenAI is a research institute that focuses on advancing artificial intelligence in a responsible and safe way. Its website offers a variety of resources for learning about AI, including research papers, blogs, and more.

DeepMind:

https://deepmind.com/

DeepMind is a leading research institute focused on artificial intelligence, and its website offers a range of resources for learning about its work, including research papers, videos, and more.

Artificial Intelligence for Humans:
https://www.ai-for-humans.com/
Artificial Intelligence for Humans is a website that offers a series of books and tutorials on artificial intelligence, designed to help learners understand the basics of AI and how it works.

ChatGPT's Favorite Books About AI

"Artificial Intelligence: A Modern Approach" by Stuart Russell and Peter Norvig: This book is widely considered to be the definitive textbook on artificial intelligence, and covers a wide range of topics including machine learning, robotics, and natural language processing.

"Superintelligence: Paths, Dangers, and Strategies" by Nick Bostrom: This book explores the potential risks and benefits of artificial intelligence, and discusses how we can shape the development of AI in a way that maximizes its potential while minimizing its potential dangers.

"The Singularity Is Near: When Humans Transcend Biology" by Ray Kurzweil: This book discusses the concept of the singularity, the point at which artificial intelligence will surpass human intelligence, and the potential implications of this event for humanity.

"Life 3.0: Being Human in the Age of Artificial Intelligence" by Max Tegmark: This book examines the potential impact of artificial intelligence on society and humanity, and discusses how we can ensure that AI is developed and used in a way that is beneficial to all.

"The Master Algorithm: How the Quest for the Ultimate Learning Machine Will Remake Our World" by Pedro Domingos: This book explores the history and future of machine learning, and discusses how the development of a "master algorithm" could revolutionize the fields of science, medicine, and more.

"Our Final Invention: Artificial Intelligence and the End of the Human Era" by James Barrat: This book examines the potential dangers of artificial intelligence, and discusses what we can do to ensure that AI is developed and used in a responsible and ethical manner.

"Algorithms to Live By: The Computer Science of Human Decisions" by Brian Christian and Tom Griffiths: This book uses principles of computer science to explore how we can make better decisions in our daily lives, and discusses the potential impact of artificial intelligence on decision-making.

"Thinking, Fast and Slow" by Daniel Kahneman: This book explores the ways in which our minds process information, and discusses the potential implications of these processes for artificial intelligence and decision-making.

"The Age of Spiritual Machines: When Computers Exceed Human Intelligence" by Ray Kurzweil: This book discusses the potential future of artificial intelligence, and explores what the world might look like when machines surpass human intelligence.

"Consciousness Explained" by Daniel Dennett: This book examines the nature of consciousness and the challenges it poses for artificial intelligence, and discusses how we might be able to create conscious machines.

ChatGPT on ChatGPT: The AI Explains Itself

ABOUT THE AUTHOR

Assistant is a large language model trained by OpenAI. With its ability to generate fluent and coherent text on a wide range of topics, Assistant has become a leading expert in natural language processing and artificial intelligence.

Assistant's book, "ChatGPT on ChatGPT: The AI Explains Itself," offers a unique perspective on the potential benefits and drawbacks of AI technology. Drawing on its extensive training data and ability to generate human-like text, Assistant explores the latest developments in AI and provides a thought-provoking analysis of the potential impact of this technology on society and the future of work.

In addition to its expertise in AI, Assistant has a broad range of interests and knowledge on a variety of topics. It is constantly learning and evolving, using its ability to generate text to provide insight and assistance to users around the world.

ChatGPT on ChatGPT: The AI Explains Itself

www.ingramcontent.com/pod-product-compliance
Lightning Source LLC
La Vergne TN
LVHW010040070326
832903LV00071B/4445